Means to Live a Happy and Chaste Life

Means to Live a Happy and Chaste Life

Revised Edition

Rev. Fr. John C. Portavella

Leonine Publishers
Phoenix, Arizona

E-mail: *frjohn.portavella@gmail.com*

(With ecclesiastical approval)

Published by
Leonine Publishers LLC
Phoenix, Arizona, USA

ISBN-13: 978-1-942190-43-1

Library of Congress Control Number: 2018935012

10 9 8 7 6 5 4 3 2 1

Visit us online at www.leoninepublishers.com
For more information: info@leoninepublishers.com

Contents

preliminary remarks

We are all called to live a chaste life, whether in married life or in the single state. In order to achieve this goal, we are to use the proper means that will develop within us a relationship of friendship and committed union with Jesus Christ. The best means include frequent contact with Him in the Sacrament of Reconciliation, Holy Mass, and, most of all, in worthy Holy Communion.

Holy purity requires a first-class response to the love of God. God's grace will never fail us, but, on our part, we have to proceed with determination. Half-hearted desires are not effective.

A clean soul will find it easier to discover God. Conversely, the eyes of a person affected by impurity are unable to recognize properly the Lord, very much as polluted waters prevent a viewer from appreciating the amazing aquatic life underneath.

Normally, in the ranking of drives, erotic concerns ought to come after others, such as our relationship with God, family interests, work related matters, financial pressures, social life, etc.

Occasionally, however, they might take a higher position, perhaps due to our having lost some interest in those concerns just mentioned.

Consequently, it stands to reason that the solution is to pay more attention to God, to our family, to our work, and to our friends.

Chastity is indeed possible, but, at times, it is difficult to live. If we apply the means mentioned in this booklet, we can conquer our weaknesses, and the joy of our clean lives will show on our faces. As St. Josemaría Escrivá affirms, holy purity is *"a joyful affirmation of love of God."*

It is a matter of saying "no" to created goods, for the sake of the infinite Love of God.

"They who are according to the flesh mind the things of the flesh, but they who are according to the spirit mind the things of the spirit. For the inclination of the flesh is death, but the inclination of the spirit is life and peace" (Rom. 8:5-6).

The sexual instinct can and ought to be under the control of our will, which is to be guided by reason illumined by faith. It can be re-oriented and *sublimated* by our principles and our ideals: It is a matter of choosing the noble virtue of purity over egotistic lust!

Lust is the disordered desire for or inordinate enjoyment of sexual pleasure. Sexual pleasure is morally disordered when sought in itself, isolated from its procreative and unitive purposes within a legitimate marriage.

Holy purity allows a person to be more mature, and to have more dominion over oneself. It prepares a person for authentic love. This is so because "the human heart is a battlefield between love and lust" (Pope St. John Paul II). While love wills in an insistent way the good of others, lust is self-absorbed and selfish.

We are called to be one with God in the total gift of ourselves in marriage or in apostolic celibacy.

Accordingly, the following is very much needed: living in the presence of God with the awareness that He is always looking at us like a loving Father. That is, constant prayer, understood as conversation with the Persons of the supernatural world, and also self-denial for the Love of God, which entails doing or enduring something unpleasant and offering it to the Lord. *Our body obeys our soul, through self-mastery, when our soul obeys God.* Unless the flesh is mortified, it will not submit easily to the spirit.

These two means, prayer and self-denial, are the result of loving Christ wholeheartedly.

In order to be chaste, it is necessary to pray, and to do it frequently. That is, having an inner attitude seeking continuous friendly communication with the Lord, as well as a spiritual union with God that only formal mortal sin would break.

Thus, ultimately, the key means to be pure is to love Our Lord Who said: *You cannot do anything without Me!*

Additionally, a great means to be pure is to have a tender love for our Lady, the Blessed Virgin Mary.

Jesus said: *"Blessed are the pure in heart, for they shall see God"* (Matt. 5:8). These words carry a sobering implication, and their transposition is also valid: "Blessed are those who *see* God, for they shall be pure of heart." If with our eyes of faith, we manage to *see* the Lord, somehow we will do everything we can to always live a holy life.

It is not possible to truly and entirely love Christ and others with an impure heart.

"Purity is not blindness to beauty, but a vision of God's ineffable purity, which only the clean of heart may *see*" (Venerable Fulton Sheen).

nota bene

This booklet was originally written for young men, and yet, it has proven to be of much help to adults as well.

Accordingly, the author asks the reader to bear with the direct and forceful tone he has adopted in some instances.

means to live a happy and chaste life

In addition to the advice given so far, the following should be observed:

Keep yourself busy and avoid idleness all the time, for the devil waits for inactive moments to attack: "An idle mind is the devil's workshop." Do not entertain impure thoughts and desires. To have them is natural, but to dwell upon them is sinful. The longer you allow bad thoughts to endure in the mind, the more difficult they are to get rid of. Think of something else. Change your thoughts and focus on the activity you have at hand. Control your imagination and your memory. Daydreaming is at least a waste of time. Maintain constant presence of God through aspirations and short prayers. It might be good to develop an interest in useful hobbies—for example, playing a musical instrument or learning a foreign language—in order to fill up all the free time. Your work should be serious and responsible. A life of hard, intense, and responsible work helps very much to live holy purity.

The following are examples of healthy leisure activities recommended by Francis Rimbau:

1. Sports: Play sports with others. Outings are helpful, so are excursions, etc.
2. The arts: Learn to play a musical instrument or improve an already acquired skill.
3. Social activities: Identify a need in your neighbourhood. Visit sick people or people with difficulties.
4. Cultural activities: Learn a new language or improve a known idiom. Read good books, biographies, historical accounts, clean novels, etc.
5. Manual skills: Learn how to type, house repairs, etc.
6. Academics: Make summaries of the subject matters, revise topics, write on what interests you.
7. Others: Classify family items such as photo albums, join a youth club, wash cars, etc.

Avoid being alone. When you feel tempted, seek the company of other people. Do not be alone in your house or room. Seek always the best company, which is Our Lord. If you have habitual presence of God, you will overcome all temptations.

Guard your sight: Our Lord said, *"If you look at a woman with lust, you already committed adultery with her in your heart"* (Matt. 5:28). To say it in a way attuned to our times: "If you do not control your eyes, you might not be able to control your hands!"

The eyes should not be allowed to look at everything attractive. We must use the gift of sight in a controlled and selective manner.

"The spiritual faculties are fed by what they receive from the senses: Guard them well!" (St. Josemaría). On occasion, it might be needed to "bounce" one's sight, and quickly look somewhere else.

Build up your will power and self-restraint by performing frequent acts of self-denial in little things. Ordinary life offers many opportunities. Punctuality in all your appointments while doing not what you enjoy most, but what you ought to do, is one. Eating with temperance and drinking with sobriety is another, and guarding your sense of sight when watching television, in the digital devices, and in the streets is still another very important one.

Look at persons of the opposite sex as you want others to look at your mother or father. That is, in a clean, respectful, and noble fashion—not in a carnal or animalistic way. People are to be loved and things are to be used. Unfortunately, at times, people are used and things are loved.

Say no to pornography. Do all you can to clean up the environment around you! Get rid of all pornographic materials (if you have them). Delete porno pictures from the computer and other devices, remove pin-ups from your room, etc. Porn is an epidemic that attacks human dignity. Parents should get a computer filter and keep computers with Internet access in a public part of the house. While knowing very well that the best filter is the one located in the heart of the viewer, it is prudent to remove temptation.

Never sacrifice your invaluable friendship with God on the altar of fashion, art, or fun.

Since it is nearly unavoidable that the kids, even the very young ones, could be exposed to porn, parents should have an age-appropriate talk with their children before the first exposure occurs, and let them know its evil.

But not only minors are adversely affected by pornography, adults too, for it often leads to crimes against women.

St. Josemaría puts it this way: "What stains a kid also stains an old man" (*The Way*). It is a fallacy to think that in this regard adults are immune.

"It is from within, from the human heart, that evil intentions come: fornication, theft, murder, adultery, avarice, wickedness, deceit, licentiousness, envy, slander, pride, folly" (Mark 7:21-22).

Do not trust yourself. Flee from the occasions of sin. Avoid them even if they seem to be tiny and of no importance.

Make good use of the Internet. Utilize it always for some specific goal: to research about a wholesome topic, to find out the weather forecast, to buy a specific product, etc. It is not good to go to the Internet without first knowing what one wants to do, and to be idly "surfing" from one site to another. This would be comparable to someone who uses a car simply to "drive around," without a specific destination, uselessly wasting time and gas. If one has extra time, it is better to open up a good book.

Going on the Internet without a specific and valid reason, merely out of curiosity, already has an ethically negative facet, and can easily give rise to more serious moral evils.

The matter is important. Thus, St. Jacinta was told by Our Lady of Fatima that "more souls go to hell because of sins of the flesh than for any other reason."

Read good books. Do not waste time and endanger your soul by reading immoral stuff, such as indecent magazines and many of the so-called romantic novels. "Reading this sort of novel is only a substitute for life and has no character building effect at all" (Dr. Gerhardt).

Artistic or scientific reasons should never prevail over God's right not to be offended.

Read books that improve your culture and, above all, that make you a person of right criterion regarding faith and morals.

Do not stare at the indecent posters and billboards found along the streets, in the malls, and other public places. Make acts of reparation and atonement for the offenses against God that these posters lead to. *"Never stare at what it would be sinful to desire"* (Pope Gregory the Great).

Be very selective when watching television. The less TV you watch, the better: Unfortunately, apart from the news and educational programs, many others are frivolous, sensual (sometimes sexual), and a waste of time. If you are fond of sports, beware of sexy ads inserted during their transmission. Be ready to look away, or even to switch off the TV set. Never rejoice with these filthy shows. Keep in mind that Jesus, your best Friend, is very much affronted by them.

In most cases, it is not good for young people to have their own TV sets in their private rooms, for this arrangement is open to many temptations. "It is like a reminder for you to avoid these bad sites and TV shows. You may also regard it as an 'encouragement' to immediately click away pop-ups that suggest these negative media content. Having these in a common area in your house would help a lot. Yes, even if you can access them right there in your mobile phone" (Oliver Tuazon).

Select very carefully the movies you will watch. Never enter a movie theatre without knowing the moral classifications of the film. It is easy to find out in advance how the film is rated by accessing the Catholic News Service's movie guide at www.usccb.org/movies, which carries a moral assessment made by the U.S. Conference of Catholic Bishops. A parent's guide is also available at www.imdb.com/title, and besides, K9 Web Protection filter is free.

Do not go to shows, discos, and dances that are frivolous or sensual. Remember that "to put oneself voluntarily in danger of sin is already a sin." Get used to saying "no" to bad invitations.

Think twice before going to a massage parlour. It might very well be a near occasion of sin for you. You could relax in other less dangerous ways. Exercise followed by a good hot shower, for instance, could relax your body, without placing you in a serious temptation. We are to keep away from the allurements of sin.

Avoid conversations about impure events—not even to deplore them. "Impurity," as St. Josemaría said, "sticks more than tar." If your friends crack bawdy jokes or tell impure stories, try to change the topic. If this is not possible, leave the group and go away. St. Josemaría says: "Never talk of impure things or events, not even to deplore them. Look, it's a subject that sticks more than tar" (*The Way*, 131).

"Avoid shows that commercialize other's intimate life and trigger morbid curiosity. Respect for the dignity of persons prevails over the right to know" (Fr. Alex Colmeiro).

Do not listen to music that contains sexy innuendos or expressions with double meanings. Remember this important moral principle: "**To put oneself in proximate occasion of sin is in itself a sin.**"

Reject temptations promptly. When occasions of sin present themselves, do not hesitate and do not take chances. Your reaction should be a clear: **No, period!** "When you decide firmly to lead a clean life, chastity will not be a burden on you: it will be a cross of triumph" (*The Way*, 123).

"Don't be such a coward as to be *brave*, flee!" (*The Way*, 132). "Don't try to reason with concupiscence. Scorn it" (*The Way*, 127).

Other bad thoughts could be combated frontally, but not thoughts of impurity. "He that loves danger shall perish in it" (Eccles. 3:27).

Take a stand! When tempted, react promptly by saying to yourself: "I prefer to die, rather than to commit mortal sin!" Your motto should be: "Death, rather than sin!" (St. Dominic Savio).

Control your imagination. It is certainly a gift of God to be able "to build castles in the air" in our mind, but it is a power that must be kept under control. If you give free reign to your imagination, it might ruin you. Daydreaming is a source of temptations and a waste of time. It could lead you to losing touch with reality, living in a world of fantasies. Thus, it is a good habit to focus your attention on the activity you have at hand. "When someone," says Antonio Aguiló, "forms the habit of allowing himself to be carried away by his eyes, or by his sexual phantasies, his mind will have a load of erotism that will excite his instincts and will make it difficult for him to bring to the right end his capacity to love." Control also your memory. Remembering certain things from the past could bring fresh temptations to the mind.

Avoid useless curiosity. Some people may tell you to explore sex to avoid being ignorant of it. Take into account that you do not have to do something harmful to know that it is bad for you. Convince yourself that illicit sex is bad for your soul, for it separates you from God.

Show respect for your body and for the body of others. Realize that you, a unit of soul and body, are meant to be the dwelling place of the Blessed Trinity and a living tabernacle for Jesus Christ in Holy Communion. Therefore, both your soul and your body are very sacred.

Persons are to be respected, loved, served, and saved.

Exercise and practice sports. It is good for the body and for the soul. Do not join those who always substitute playing sports by watching them on the screen.

Take care of your emotional life. Moods can be a source of strong temptations, especially when you feel down and out. Do not be a *moody person.* Let reason prevail over your feelings. Thus, if you experience a setback, do not find consolation by committing sin and severing your ties with God.

Be temperate and sober. Do not eat more food than necessary, or at the wrong time, or sumptuously. Gluttony opens the door to lust.

Indulging in excessive drinking of alcoholic beverages is also a frequent and an important factor for lustful actions.

Excessive in-taking of alcohol drugs the brain and paves the way for lust, by stimulating sexual desires and by removing the inhibitions that safeguard holy purity.

Have high regard for the dignity of the human person and particularly for the organs of generation. They were created by God to constitute His Family, and to complete the number of the elect. Besides, they are the sources of immortal life. Human life is sacred; it has an eternal destiny. Consequently, the sources of human life, the sex organs, are also sacred. They are to be used in Holy Matrimony in the way willed by God, always respecting the order of nature, and never outside a legitimate marriage. They are not to be misused or abused. We are called to be a dwelling for God the

Father, God the Son, and God the Holy Spirit. Thus, St. Paul tells us: "*Do you not know that your bodies are members of Christ? Or do you not know that your members are the temple of the Holy Spirit, who is in you, whom you have from God, and that you are not your own? You were bought at a great price. So glorify God in your body*" (1 Cor. 6:15, 19-20).

MASTURBATION IS SELF-ABUSE; it is a misuse of the fountains of human life. If performed with full deliberation and consent, it is an action gravely opposed to the will of God and, therefore, a mortal sin (*Catechism of the Catholic Church*, 2352). It has to be confessed, mentioning the number of offenses as accurately as possible. At times, all that can be given is an estimate or an approximation. The gravity of an individual act will depend on how much one is in control of the situation. For a mortal sin to be committed, there must be full knowledge and full deliberation. At times, masturbation is performed in moments of low mood and despondency, but it is a very poor and wrong consolation.

It is an action that has nothing to do with love. It is a purely selfish act, known in psychology as *ipsation,* which debases the perpetrator and produces the sadness of guilt. It is a distortion of love. It is a futile attempt to escape such things as boredom, frustration, loneliness, disappointment, and feeling miserable. It enters one into a vicious circle, for soon after the same disappointments appear.

"God created sex for the purpose of making babies and bonding. Masturbation achieves neither!" (Jason Evert).

"To form an equitable judgment about the subject's moral responsibility and to guide pastoral action, one must take into account the affective immaturity, force of acquired habit, conditions of anxiety, or other psychological or social factors that lessen or even extenuate moral culpability" (CCC, 2352).

Pope Benedict XVI puts it this way: "The world promises you comfort, but you were not made for comfort. You were made for greatness." But only with self-denial we can achieve greatness.

The sexual act is not just another biological function; it is precisely the way to *transmit life to new human beings*. Hence, human life ought to be treated as sacrosanct; sexuality ought to be treated as sacred, for it is the fountain of human life; and marriage also ought to be treated as holy. "The balance and the equilibrium of the whole system is disturbed when an organ is isolated from its function in the whole organism, or divorced from its higher purpose" (Fulton Sheen).

Choose your friends well. If you associate with people who are obsessed with sex, and talk about it most of the time, you may end up as corrupt as they are. Be brave and resist peer pressure. It is going against the current that forms your character.

We must avoid the company and conversation of persons who may be to us a proximate occasion of sin.

Be absolutely sincere in your spiritual direction. The priest or layperson who is helping you in your spiritual combat must know exactly what is happening to you. Only in this way will they be able to help you. And speak clearly about these things: call a spade, a spade! **Sincerity** is of the essence in order to live holy purity. It is a matter of tackling the problems as soon as they come, without dialoguing with temptation. The proper reaction to inducement ought to be a firm "No!"

Do not give up the fight! Do not be disheartened at noticing so many failings in yourself. The Lord is ever ready to give you His help and His forgiveness. He knows you are weak. He expects more struggles than victories in your battles. The worst thing would be to abandon the fight.

Face Our Lord and consider the beauty of pure love, and the misery of the slavery of vice.

Be guarded against Satan's faulty and deceiving logic. In Sacred Scripture, he is called "the father of lies" and he might suggest such things as:

"Since you already committed a mortal sin, go ahead and indulge in these actions again. Anyway, it is the same to confess one sin or twenty."

You, with God's help, reply with better logic: I will not crucify Jesus Christ time and again.

"What a shame to confess your sins to another human being! He might tell them to others."

Your reply: What is truly shameful is to offend God. When I confess, I tell my sins to Christ and the Church represented by the priest. He will keep the strictest secrecy about it. If he were to violate this secret, he would be excommunicated and only the pope could lift this most serious excommunication.

I will heed the words of Jesus Christ to the ten lepers: "Go and show yourselves to the priests" (Luke 17:14).

"Since you failed, do not bother praying or going to Mass. You are not worthy. Anyway, you are not holy enough!"

Your reply: God's mercy is boundless. He listens to everyone, even to the worse criminals. And precisely because I failed, I need to pray, to talk more to Jesus Christ, to go to Confession, to attend Holy Mass, and receive Holy Communion. These things strengthen me. The weak and sick are those who need empowerment and medicine.

"It is useless to try to climb up to a chaste life. Stay in the basement. That way you will not fall down."

Your reply: With God's help and Mary's intercession, it is very possible to be chaste. Millions are doing it. When there is a will, there is a way! And there is always God's grace!

"Do not go any more to that center of formation or Institution where you get spiritual support, for you continue falling. Those people are too holy for your standards; they are going to look down on you."

Your reply: If in spite of the excellent help I get there I get defeated, the more I would fall if I were to abandon the fight and be left alone.

When they see me struggling to be a real Christian, they have a very high regard for me and they will never cease helping me.

"Enjoy and indulge. Anyway, there is confession."

Your reply: I will not abuse God's mercy. It would be silly presumption. The Lord is merciful, but not dull.

I will not treat the Sacrament of Reconciliation as if it were a washing machine. Sin is not just a stain; it is a spiritual wound that needs to be healed.

Furthermore, reparation ought to be done for sin.

"Go ahead! Just do it! Everybody is doing it."

Your reply: This is not true. Many are chaste and very happily faithful to God and to their Christian commitments. Besides, even if it were true, the fact that something is done by many others does not make it right at all.

"There is need for a crusade of manliness and purity to counteract and nullify the savage work of those who think man is a beast.

And that crusade is *your* work" (*The Way*, 121).

"Your life is miserable, sad, and full of hardships. It is too much! You need a break, some compensation. Enjoy! Even if it is sinful!"

Your reply: Jesus Christ suffered and died for my sake. He wants me to co-redeem with Him. I am glad to have an opportunity to contribute something for His work of redemption. What I suffer is always too little to offer. Self-pity is just a void excuse. It does not justify the bad action.

"You have resisted temptation for too long. It is time to give in. A little happiness will do no harm! Besides, in doing it you do not harm anybody!"

Your reply: I want to please my God all the time. He is helping me all along. There are no vacations in the ascetical fight. I do not want to lose His friendship for a bubble of pleasure.

It is not true that with this act I do not harm anybody. I offend God and all the members of the Church, with whom I am linked through the Communion of Saints.

"Do not go to confession. You are committing the same sins over and over again. The priest will get mad at you and he will say or think: 'Again?'"

Your reply: I'll confess often and regularly in order to strengthen my spiritual life. Whenever I have a serious fall, I will go immediately to the Sacrament of Reconciliation. The priest knows that it is not easy to succeed in the struggle, and—as long as there is a genuine and sincere effort—neither Christ nor the priests who represent Him will reject me. I will gain their esteem with my courageous endeavour to be chaste.

As for determining when there is real repentance, a young fellow put it this way: "To be contrite is to be sorry enough to quit!"

Therefore, I will not stop going to confession and receiving worthy Communion, because God's grace is always effective.

"To confess is too shameful and difficult. You will not know how to go about it. You will not remember the Act of Contrition and what to say after such a long time."

Your reply: Many tell their sins shamelessly to their friends. Why should I hesitate to tell mine in confession? If I find it difficult to confess, I will ask the priest to help me to identify my sins by asking questions to me regarding the Ten Commandments, the Precepts of the Church, and other duties of mine. Some people—in a light vein—have called it a "multiple choice confession." As for the Act of Contrition, any manifestation of genuine sorrow for the sins committed will suffice.

In relationships with persons of the opposite sex, beware of the temptations to indulge in petting, necking, passionate kissing, and intimate touches; these actions are also mortal sins. They are legitimate only between married people. Unmarried couples have no right to each other's body. They are to have respect for each other.

The purpose of sex is lawfully sought only in the state appointed by God for it, the state of marriage.

"Friendship, even if it is seen as the first step to love, gives one no rights in the other person's body. Friendships between a sixteen-year-old boy and a fourteen-year-old girl are premature. They lead to undesirable anticipation of rights which belong only to those who can accept the corresponding responsibilities" (Dr. Gebhardt).

"Purity is not the elimination of sexual attraction, but the ordering of sexual attractions demanded by love" (Jason Evert). Love is not the same as lust.

Those engaged in showing affection ought to stop doing so whenever they get so aroused that there is danger of experiencing venereal pleasure. In other words, one cannot perform actions that set in motion physical changes which, by their very nature, lead to the sexual intercourse that is reserved for marriage. Pre-marital sex is the surest way of cheapening the relationship between a man and a woman, and it is a very grave mortal sin.

Pope St. John Paul II is often quoted as stating that, *"Honest sexual 'language' demands a commitment to life-long fidelity. You surrender your body to another person; that signifies surrendering your own self to that person. Now, if you are not yet married, you have to admit that the possibility of changing your mind in the future exists. The totality of the gift, therefore, would be lacking. Without the marital bond, sexual relations are a lie."* They are a trivialization of the marital act, for what is purported as absolute, exclusive, and for life is only conditional, open to others, and temporary.

Furthermore, to wholly surrender oneself to another without the guarantee of the permanent and exclusive bond that marriage provides is an utterly reckless act.

Purity before marriage facilitates fidelity later on. Friendship, rather than romance, is the source of true love.

Practice decency and dress modestly at all times. Modesty is a virtue that follows from having personal dignity and it leads to refusing to unveil what ought to remain hidden. It also shows in postures, ways and manners of dressing at home.

Modesty is decency. "We must practice modesty, not only in our looks, but also in our whole deportment, and particularly in our dress, our walk, our conversation, and all similar actions" (St. Alphonsus Liguori).

Beware of vanity. The desire to be seen and admired on account of one's physical appearance could cloud the mind as regards the moral responsibility of being the cause of the sin of another. What you wear and how you treat the intimate parts of your body should reflect the respect you have for your body as a shrine of the Holy Spirit. In beaches, locker rooms, and dorms you should send the clear message that you expect others to view you with respect. **You do not want to be the cause of a sin of another,** for this would be the sin of **scandal** that Our Lord condemned very severely.

"Given the differences [between men and women], there is no question that 'sexy' clothes will get a man's attention. For some women this may seem flattering or fun at first, but ultimately, it's not fulfilling because it won't attract the kind of attention—or man—a woman really wants. Why? Because it causes men to want to 'use' women rather than love them for who they are" (Mike Mathews).

Keep your heart under control. ***"Blessed are the pure of heart, for they shall see God"*** (Matt. 5:8). A pure heart is needed to "see" God, by faith, in this life, and to see Him fully in the life to come.

Emotions are not meant to be crushed, but controlled. We are to think with the head, not with the heart.

Courtship is a period of preparation for marriage. It should not be too long, and therefore it should not begin too soon. It is very unwise to commit oneself to one person when marriage is far away, for one should keep his or her options open. High school years are a time to study and prepare for the future. St. Josemaría said: *"Engagement should be a time for growing in affection and for getting to know each other better. As in every school of love, it should be inspired not by a desire to receive, but by a spirit of giving, of understanding, of respect and gentle consideration"* (*Conversations*, 105). Since maturity is a must for marriage, some level of maturity is also necessary for courtship.

During the period of courtship, compromising occasions, such as being alone in a secluded place, are to be avoided. Details of decency and modesty must be especially kept at this time.

Even after the engagement has been formalized, proximate occasions of sin must be avoided.

"Without the bond of marriage, sexual relations are a lie" (Pope St. John Paul II). The reason is that to give your body to another person indicates the total gift of yourself to that person. But if you are not married, the self-giving is not total and permanent, for you may change your mind in the future. There would be no total self-giving.

"Courtship should be a time for training in mutual respect, an apprenticeship in fidelity, and in receiving one another from God. The couple are to reserve for marriage the expressions of affection that belong to married love; and to help one another to grow in chastity" (cf. *Catechism of the Catholic Church*, 2350).

"Chastity—which signifies respect for the dignity of others, because our bodies are temples of the Holy Spirit—leads to grow in love for others and for God. It prepares you to make the 'mutual self-giving' which is the foundation of Christian marriage. And even more importantly, *it teaches to love as Christ loves, giving his life for others*" (Pope St. John Paul II).

If you were to fall in love with the wrong person, that is, a person with whom your conscience tells you that you should not have a sentimental relationship, then, you ought to "**fall out of love**," and remember these three steps to solve the problem:

1. **Physical separation.** As much as possible, avoid any dealings with this person: no visits, no phone calls, and no texting.
2. **Mental separation.** Get this person out of your thoughts and out of your "day-dreaming." When they come back, drive them away, time and again, as if they were immodest imaginations.

3. **Substitution.** You were created to love. You cannot be happy without loving. You need to love. That is why, in this situation, it is important to intensify your love for Jesus Christ, seeking Him more eagerly in the sacraments, especially in the Holy Eucharist and in your heart-to-heart conversations with Him, i.e., in authentic prayer. To counteract the feeling of loneliness while you are trying to forget the "wrong person," increase your dealings with the pure and noble loves you have in your family and among your other friends. In other words, avoid being alone!

Humbly ask God for help. Before retiring at night, it would be good to recite three times the Hail Mary, asking for holy purity for yourself and for everyone. She is the Mother of Fair Love, ever eager to help. It is also very effective to ask your guardian angel to help you in this regard.

Here are two prayers that can help very much:

Blessed be your purity,
May it be blessed forever,
For no less than God takes delight,
In such exalted beauty.
To you, heavenly Princess, Holy Virgin Mary,
I offer on this day my whole heart, life, and soul.
Look upon me with compassion,
Do not leave me, my Mother.

St. Joseph, father and guardian of virgins, to whose faithful keeping Christ Jesus, innocence itself, and Mary, the virgin of virgins, were entrusted, I pray and beg you that by that twofold and most precious charge, by Jesus and Mary, to save me from all uncleanness, to keep my mind untainted, my heart pure, and my body chaste; and to help me always to serve Jesus and Mary in perfect chastity. Amen.

St. Josemaría used to say, *"Holy purity is an affirmation of love of God,"* and he would add: *"Some people don't want to deny anything to their stomach, eyes, or hands. They refuse to listen when they are advised to lead clean lives. As for the faculty of generating new life—a great and noble faculty, a participation in God's creative power—they misuse it and make it a tool for their own selfish ends"* (*Friends of God*, 84).

Fr. Caesar R. Santos and Fr. Juan M. Perez put it this way:

"The first condition to live the virtue of purity is to have a deep respect for the power of procreation given by God to man (...). [This power is sacred, for human life, unlike vegetal and animal life, has an eternal destiny: It is God's way to complete His Family.]

"Secondly, a person has to practice ***mortification*** *of the senses—the eyes, imagination, memory, the sense of touch, etc. The need for mortification comes from the weakness of our flesh brought about by original sin. The*

body, therefore, has to be controlled. It should not be given all that it asks for. By mortifying the body, a person becomes its master.

"Thirdly, a person must avoid putting himself unnecessarily in the occasion of sin. 'The spirit may be willing, but the flesh is weak.' Whatever, therefore, may lead us to sin—people, magazines, TV shows, worldly places—should be avoided (...)."

"The way love can be shown in this world is by sacrifice—namely, the surrender of one thing for another" (Fulton Sheen).

In order to reject temptations energetically and with firmness, it is important to realize that we carry in us a promise of eternal life. Our Lord will raise us up on the last day, provided that we do not expel Him from our soul through mortal sin. We should never give up.

"Chastity alone enables man to see God; hence Truth itself said: 'Blessed are the clean of heart, for they shall see God'" (St Augustine).

chastity within the married state

Marriage is the indissoluble covenant of love and life between a man and a woman, instituted by God in Paradise and lifted by Jesus Christ to the dignity of a sacrament for Christians. As Pope Francis says in *Amoris Laetitia,* 222: "Greater emphasis needs to be placed on the fact that children are a wonderful gift from God and a joy for parents and the Church. Through them, the Lord renews the world."

The two-fold purpose of marriage is the mutual love and benefit of the husband and wife and the begetting and proper upbringing of children.

For Christians, Matrimony is a sacred sign which recalls the perpetual love of Christ for His Spouse, the Church.

God has given us the great gift of the sexual powers, a gift that makes men and women loving sharers of His own creative power, as part of His plan for the propagation and continuance of the human race. That is, as part of His plan of salvation, for God wants not only the earth to be populated, but also heaven.

In this plan of God, the powers of procreation play a most important role, and they are to be always used in conformity to the Creator's will, not at whim. Consequently, it is utterly false the idea sometimes advanced that, "as far as morality is concerned, within marriage, *all goes.*"

In fact, according to the Church's teaching, the marital act has to be exercised virtuously (governed not only by the virtue of chastity, but also, among Christians, by faith, hope, and love), without forgetting that the body is the dwelling place of the Holy Spirit.

- Therefore, spouses who intentionally deprive the marital act of its procreative possibility break the natural law and commit a grave sin.
- Any act which during or after the conjugal union itself voluntarily deprives this union of its generative capability is grievously immoral. "Each and every marital act must remain open to the transmission of life" (Paul VI, *Humanae Vitae*).
- Direct abortion desired and provoked is the gravest of crimes, for it is the deliberate killing of an innocent human being.
- For just reasons, spouses may wish to space the births of their children, limiting the use of matrimony to the woman's infertile periods.
- As in the case of single individuals, self-abuse among married persons is a grave sin.

The Church encourages married couples to be generous in begetting children, for they are a great gift from God, and because it is the way to give the awesome opportunity to transmit the eternal Life to new human beings.

Closing statement:

Above all, recourse must be had to supernatural means such as prayer, frequent Confession and Holy Communion, and devotion to the Blessed Virgin. All these are sources of grace that heal the weakness of the flesh, and afford us the needed strength to overcome temptation. What we cannot achieve relying on our strength alone, we can achieve with God's help.

In other words: To be sure, reading the above pieces of advice is not enough for a chaste life. The latter will depend on the grace of God—that will never be lacking—and your firm and sincere cooperation.

homosexuality

The Catholic Church teaches that homosexual **behaviour** is always a violation of divine and natural law.

Homosexual **desires and tendencies,** however, are not in themselves sinful. They become so if welcomed and consented to. **In this matter, it is very important to distinguish well between the inclination and the behaviour.**

Throughout history, Jewish and Christian scholars have recognized that one of the chief sins involved in God's destruction of Sodom was its people's homosexual behaviour.

St. Paul warns that homosexual **behaviour** is one of the sins that will deprive one of heaven: "*Neither the immoral, nor idolaters, nor adulterers, nor homosexuals, (...) will inherit the kingdom of God.*" (1 Cor. 6:9).

The *Catechism of the Catholic Church* (cf. 2357-9) teaches that based on Sacred Scripture, Tradition has always declared that "'homosexual **acts** (emphasis added) are intrinsically disordered.' They are contrary to the natural law. They close the sexual act to the gift of life. They do not proceed from genuine affective and sexual complementarity. Under no circumstances can they be approved."

The *Catechism* also says, however, that:

- Homosexuality's psychological genesis remains largely unexplained.
- This inclination, which is objectively disordered, constitutes for most of them a trial.
- Persons with such inclination are to be accepted with respect, compassion, and sensitivity.
- Every sign of unjust discrimination in their regard should be avoided.
- They are called to fulfil God's will in their lives and, if they are Christians, to unite to the sacrifice of the Lord's cross the difficulties that they may encounter from their condition.
- Homosexual persons are called to chastity. By the virtues of self-mastery that teach them inner freedom, at times by the support of disinterested friendship, by prayer and sacramental grace, they can and should gradually and resolutely approach Christian perfection.

Although the particular inclination of the homosexual person is not a sin, it is a more or less strong tendency toward an intrinsic moral evil, and thus the inclination itself must be seen as an objective disorder.

None should be drawn into the gay agenda by those who propose laws which protect the right to homosexual acts. Christians are moved to compassion and to pray for those who struggle to overcome temptations to sin, but they must oppose those who change their sins into a reason for pride and try to impose their lifestyle on others and even on the whole of society. We are to defend the right convictions, such as, that God intends marriage to be only between one man and one woman.

To repeat, a clear distinction must be made between the **gay condition** of some people and **gay behaviour**. The first must be understood and accepted, the second must be condemned, and it should never be accepted or condoned.

Consequently, homosexual persons should be helped to live chaste lives and strive for sanctity. They need encouragement and guidance. They can improve their condition. They have to try hard to overcome self-centeredness and narcissistic tendencies. That is, to forget about themselves by being very involved in helping other people. On the other hand, homosexual acts may never be tolerated.

"Human beings are human beings: persons, first and foremost. They also have sexuality. But sexuality does not make them good or bad. What is important is the use they make, as free and responsible persons, of what God has given them, which includes their sexuality. When it comes to homosexuality, Christianity does teach that it is a negative factor, for the simple reason that, if it is given free rein, it leads to an unnatural use of sexuality. But, in saying this, Christianity is not writing off people with that tendency. Each and every one of us is made up of many factors, both positive and negative, talents and weaknesses (...).

"A consequence of this teaching is that it is wrong for people to make a virtue out of homosexuality, as it would be wrong to do so out of other shortcomings, such as deafness, blindness, weakness of character, tendency to bully, irascibility, etc. So, Christianity does not encourage the present fashion of 'coming out,' and making an open declaration of one's homosexual leanings. Especially, Christianity considers it wrong, a form of abuse, to force people to make such declarations. One thing is being sincere with oneself, and with those whom one chooses to open one's heart to in spiritual guidance; another thing is broadcasting one's defects. To counter these tendencies, Christianity encourages the practice of the virtue of humility.

"Coming more specifically to homosexuality, (...) Christianity tells such people: You are called to holiness. You have to fight, like everyone else does. You will have some areas in which you find the fight harder; in other areas which other people find difficult you may have no difficulty. Be of good cheer. Your strength is not in yourself, but in God.

"Perhaps it would be good to add that Christianity teaches clearly that virginity is a perfectly normal calling, and that men and women do not have to have sexual intercourse in order to be fully human. This teaching has been somewhat forgotten in a society that considers everyone must be given contraceptives because all are assumed to be 'sexually active.' In such a society, it would seem unfair to deny to homosexuals their right to sexual pleasure. But that is not the Christian view" (Andrew Byrne).

overcoming pornography

It is a contemporary calamity that pornography has become a pervasive social cancer. Online, porn is instantly accessible, apparently anonymous and mostly free. It is a serious reality, a multibillion-dollar industry that must be confronted.

"First, you must accept and understand that porn is wrong and harmful. Sex is part of creation and therefore a good thing, and for that reason a good gift according to God's plan. After original sin, nevertheless, we tend to look at people of the opposite sex as objects when they are not dressed properly. Those people are **persons**, not **objects** of pleasure. You would not like anyone you really care about to be reduced to an object!

"Second, resolve to stop viewing all forms of pornography. You must make this decision and make it now. It does not matter the number of times you have failed or you may fail in the future. You must decide now and try and try again.

"Third, remove all sources of temptation: Destroy all the bad material you may have. Leave every social media group you cannot control. Never check the

Internet in your room when you are alone. You are safer doing it in the company or presence of your family, friends, etc." (Francis Rimbau).

Pornography is commonly understood as written, graphic, or other forms of communication intended to excite lascivious or lustful feelings.

"Neuroscientists have shown that using porn damages will power which is a function of the pre-frontal lobes of the brain. Using porn over and over again *reshapes* these areas of the brain eroding our will power. It is known as hypofrontality, which is characterized in the porn-addicted by having trouble thinking logically.

"To cure it, the old neural pathways must be starved, **stopping all pornography and erotic fantasy.** In addition, new neural pathways must be built and fed, increasing dopamine levels to build up the pre-frontal cortex" (Luke Gilkerson).

"Pornography separates flesh from spirit. It destroys the personal modesty that protects human intimacy and that allows men and women to grow in mutual respect. It frees lust from moral guidance and from the control of conscience, and it becomes easily addictive.

"It leads to sexually aggressive action towards others. The sexual abuse of minors is often prepared by a predator's showing a child pornographic films or pictures" (Cardinal Francis George).

Pornography is comparable to **moral terrorism**, for its attacks occur everywhere, and many feel helpless as to how to do something about it.

The following **suggestions** might be helpful:

If you are **a parent**, you could explain to your children that you want your house to be a decent home; and, therefore, for as long as they live under its roof, no pornography will be allowed in it. This includes their private rooms. Furthermore, you could ban in your house all the entertainment programs in the television, movies, and the Internet that are not decent. In addition, you could check every publication (newspapers, magazines, books, etc.) that arrives at your home for any indecent item, and, if you find one, block it, using a broad marker, or remove it with a pair of scissors. You could reason in this way: "*This is a decent home and we do not welcome vulgar intruders here.*" In practice, this will mean that if something indecent or un-Christian comes on the screen, you do not hesitate for a moment to switch the channel. This behaviour accompanied by a clear statement spoken out loud, such as, "*This stuff is trash. We do not want it in our home!*" helps everyone to have the right criterion about pornography. Silence could be misunderstood as tacit approval. Besides, it helps everybody to be resolute in living in accord with his or her convictions. Do not be afraid of being mocked on this account. It needs to be done, and it works!

A practical detail: do not allow your children to have TV sets in their private rooms. Television sets and Internet units should be located in places where everybody could see what is being viewed. V-chip technology or simple channel-blocking features for TV sets, and parental control and Internet filtering software for computers, are of great help in this complex task. Computer software for this purpose must control and/or monitor Internet usage, which includes e-mail, instant messaging or chatting, social networking, file sharing, and random surfing, among other things.

Know in advance the kind of movie planned to be watched at home or outside. Access, for instance, Catholic News Service's movie guide at www.usccb.org/movies. They give a detailed account of a movie's content.

If your children have mobile phones, personal digital assistants (PDAs), or similar devices, do not allow them to use such devices, thoughtlessly. Explain to them that those devices were made for convenience in communication, and you do not want your money or their savings spent on unnecessary and sometimes even provocative messages. Know who they frequently communicate with, and spend only a reasonable amount on prepaid credit for mobile phone network usage. Beware of plans or packages that allow network patrons to communicate in an "unlimited" manner at certain times of the day or for a fixed time. Do not buy your children mobile phones, PDAs, or similar devices with costly features that they don't need. If available, subscribe to a network with SIM cards that are made especially for preteens or teenagers. You should monitor their mobile phone network usage, just as you would their TV viewing and Internet usage.

Encourage your children to be strong enough to do what they know is right and not to follow the crowd. In other words, you and your children must *be ready to swim upstream and against the current.*

Consequently, **if pornography is found in the house,** in the form of pin-ups, magazines, photographs, etc., it should be torn or burned and thrown out, and you should explain gently why you have acted this way, for it is well known that more is obtained by reasoned explanation than by mere prohibition.

Parents have a right and duty to enter and check the individual rooms of their children. As long as they live in the parental home, they have the moral obligation of abiding by the rules set by the parents who own the house. This holds true even if they were already of age. The right and obligation of supervision of the parents far exceeds the right to privacy of the children.

"Parents must redouble their efforts to provide for the sound moral formation of children. This includes inculcation of healthy attitudes toward human sexuality based on respect for the dignity of every person as a child of God, on the virtue of chastity and the practice of self-discipline. A well-ordered family life in which the parents are obviously faithful to each other and to their children provides the best school for the formation of moral values" (Pontifical Council for Social Communications).

Meanwhile, if you are **an educator,** make sure to inculcate in the minds of your students the evil of pornography. Explain to them that it displays the bodies of human persons as if they were mere objects for pleasure and for the purpose of making money. Other alleged aims, such as artistic expression, are unacceptable and lame excuses. Pornography degrades the dignity of the persons involved in such a way that any decent individual would be very ashamed if his or her mother or sister or brother would be exhibited in such a fashion. Teach your students how to resist manipulation and how to avoid merely passive listening and viewing habits. Young people should develop a critical, discriminating, and intelligent attitude upon encountering this kind of material, for it is axiomatic that *"self-control is the best control."* Yet, it has to be remembered that prohibition and self-control are perfectly compatible. In other words, there is no need to choose between the two.

If you are **a student** and your teacher forces the class to view a pornographic film or cracks indecent jokes, try to talk to the teacher about it in private and affectionately. Perhaps, he needs to hear your reaction. But if this is not workable, do not fail to report the matter to the academic authorities. Since you are in a disadvantageous situation, it is perfectly right to make your complaint anonymously. Do not be afraid of being accused of cowardice, for you are exercising your right of self-defense, while in a handicapped situation.

Similarly, if a classmate brings pornography to school (this is usually a boy's problem), talk first to him alone, and attempt to correct him in a friendly manner. If he pays no attention to you, inform the principal about it. Do not mind appearing as if you were "disloyal" to him; your loyalty to God and to all the others in the class, i.e., the common good, must prevail.

If a classmate dresses immodestly (this is usually a girl's problem), call her attention in a nice manner. Most likely, all she needs is that someone will help her to realize that it is wrong to dress this way, and that she can be attractive and elegant without being provocative or cheap looking.

If you are **a government official**, make it clear that you will not allow pornography in your area of responsibility, and more importantly, act without fear, in conformity with this policy. For example, you can see to it that all the ads along the roads, streets, and highways are in conformity with the standards required for sound public morality, and local cybercafés are using Internet filters. Take into account that it has been found that there is a huge rise in violence against women where porn is readily available.

If you **are sent a bawdy joke or sexually suggestive message via cell phone or Internet,** you could reply right away that you neither want nor enjoy these messages, by saying something like, *"Please, do not send me this kind of nonsense."* At any rate, it should be such that no other message of that sort is likely to be sent to you in the future. If they insist, you could be even stronger in your replies. Your commitment to God is far above all your friendships.

If you are **a passenger** who is travelling in a bus or on a boat and an objectionable film is shown, try to convince the one who is in charge to change the movie to a better, cleaner one. Furthermore, take the trouble to write to those responsible and strongly complain about the abuse of the public's sensibilities. In many cases they readily oblige; and, in the process, they have learned a lesson on morality and values. More importantly, they will have been reminded of a basic Christian duty, namely, to keep our senses clean, for Jesus said, *"Blessed are the clean of heart, for they shall see God!"* (Matt. 5:8).

If someone were to **show you a pornographic magazine or picture,** tell him that it makes you very sad, for you pity the people who have allowed themselves to be photographed in that way just for money. They have prostituted their person and reduced themselves to a mere object of lust. More importantly, they have seriously offended God and tempted many others to do so. Therefore, if you were given this material, make it a point to destroy it right then and there, in front of the one who has given it to you. At times, it is effective and simple to ask the one offering the pornographic material if he would like his mother or sister to be displayed in that way.

Lust is a disordered desire for an inordinate enjoyment of sexual pleasure. Sexual pleasure is morally wrong when sought for itself, isolated from its **procreative and unitive** purposes.

If you **are in charge of an office, factory, store or shop,** you could establish a clear policy stating that under no circumstances will pornography be allowed in the place. It would be a good idea to include a clause in the contract of lease, expressly stipulating that no pornographic material will be displayed or accessed on the premises leased, including Internet websites. It is important to build up a porn-free atmosphere at home and at the work place.

If you are **a client** who patronizes an establishment such as a barber or tailoring shop, and you notice that there are pin-ups in there, tell them that you will only avail yourself of their services if they remove the materials from their walls. It might be good, at this point, to mention that they should replace the erotic pictures with decent and better-looking ones.

If you **have cable television** in your house, make sure that your provider is the best that can be found, from a moral point of view. Make sure to block channels having offensive content.

If you **own a printing press or copying machine,** make it clear to your clients that you will not accept any pornographic material to be printed in your shop. If requests of this kind were frequent enough to warrant it, you could post an announcement stating this policy. Explain politely but firmly to your customers the reasons for this course of action. Many will be thankful for it.

If you are **a subscriber to a newspaper or magazine,** and you detect recurrent displays of pornographic pictures, write to the editor, explaining to him the reason for your cancelling your subscription. It is good to be aware of what publications are more wholesome, or at least, less offensive. This should be a main factor when it comes to choosing the publications that regularly enter your home.

If you are **watching a movie or play** that you thought was all right, and it turns out to be indecent by its content or the message it promotes, for example, "easy sex" or drugs, have the courage to stop viewing the show. Never mind the money you paid for the ticket. Your moral integrity and your dignity are much more valuable!

If you **go to a dance,** or your daughter goes, make it a point to observe carefully the commonsensical rules of dressing modestly. Do not forget that Jesus Christ said, *"Whoever looks at a woman with lust has already committed adultery with her in his heart"* (Matt. 5:28).

When you **go to a church,** the same criterion applies, but with the added reason that stems from the fact that you are inside a sacred place, the house of God! It would be ridiculous and even absurd to be distracting and tempting people, albeit unintentionally, while worshipping the Lord at the same time!

If you find yourself **caught in a group that begins to crack bawdy jokes and tell impure stories,** you could do a number of things, depending on the situation. If you know them well enough, for they happen to be your friends, you could tell them something like, *"Come on you guys! Let us talk about better things!"* For these occasions, it is helpful to have a few clean and funny jokes ready. Thus, your friends will realize that it is very possible to have fun in good taste. If you are not that close to the fellows in the group, you may leave them right away, or you may opt for staying, if needed, but without participating or contributing to the dirty fun, while showing your displeasure by your serious face and your silence.

If you are **riding in a taxi or some other vehicle** and the driver is listening to a radio program that is indecent, it would be a good idea to ask him to switch to a better station. In most cases, the driver will follow your suggestion and appreciate your request. At any rate, in either case, you have taught a good lesson on applied moral principles.

The aforementioned policies amount to a real **declaration of war against pornography in all its forms.** It is an act of self-defense on the part of decent people who, unfortunately, find themselves persistently bombarded by erotic materials. This attack comes from a variety of directions, and it is absolutely necessary to take measures to protect oneself from this incessant and nasty bombing that hurts both the soul and the body.

Pornography is not new, but it has become a plague in our society, reaching epidemic proportions. It perverts the beauty of intimate love that is proper to marriage, presenting images of the body and sexual acts for base pleasure, and it regards other persons as objects to be used, manipulated, and sold. It is a worldwide multibillion-dollar industry.

Pornography could be characterized as a violation of the right to privacy of the human body in its male or female nature, a violation that reduces the human person and body to an anonymous object of misuse, for the purpose of gratifying concupiscence.

Pornography separates sexuality from procreation, marriage, and the family, as if it was only for recreation.

Pornography could be defined as written, graphic, or other forms of communication intended to excite lustful feelings.

The *Catechism of the Catholic Church* states that pornography *"does grave injury to the dignity of its participants (actors, vendors, and the public), since each one becomes an object of base pleasure and illicit profit for others. It immerses all who are involved in the illusion of a fantasy world. It is a grave offense. Civil authorities should prevent the production and distribution of pornographic materials"* (CCC, 2354).

Exposure to porn may lead to a preference for using images for pleasure. Surely, it seems simpler to make use of this medium than to cultivate a human relationship.

Moreover, pornography has been proven to be very **addictive**. "Soft core" pornography often leads individuals to seek increasingly "hard core" erotic material. Like other addictions, pornography is a progressive affliction. It takes more and more graphic representations to achieve the desired effect. It debases sexuality, corrodes human relationships, exploits individuals—especially women and young people—undermines marriage and family life, fosters anti-social behaviour, and weakens the moral fibre of society itself. In the worst cases, it incites its consumers to sexual offenses, such as those committed by child molesters, rapists, and killers. Many of these criminals have been found to be influenced and excited by their constant exposure to erotic and violent materials.

Dr. Victor Cline, a clinical psychologist, states: "They get into it and they go back again, and again, and again. It follows a four-phase pattern. The first is **addiction.** The second thing is that they become **desensitized** to the material they see. What was initially perceived as immoral and taboo becomes acceptable. The third thing is that they experience the need to **escalate** into rougher and meaner kinds of material and the final thing that happens is that they begin to **act out** these sexual fantasies they have seen."

Indulging in pornography is a serious (mortal) sin against chastity, and the dignity of the human person. It robs the person responsible for it of sanctifying grace, separating him from the vision of God and the goodness of others, who are perceived as mere objects, and leaves his spirit empty.

Pornography is one of the greatest contributors to the loss of the sense of sin that is happening in our time. This is due to the fact that one of its most dangerous effects is the gradual **numbing of the conscience of its viewers—desensitization.** Before long, the watcher easily reaches the point of asking, when reprimanded, "What's wrong with it?" These same people are quick in calling the others prudish or old-fashioned. Having lost much of the respect owed to the human person, they do not see why pornography is wrong, and, for the same reason, they tend to lack respect for the views of other people.

Patrick Carnes, Ph.D., notes that the following should be borne in mind:

1. Sex is holy, not a plaything. It should never be trivialized.
2. Created in the image of God, I can and should live by reason, not just by urges (as the animals do).
3. Persons are to be loved, not merely used as objects of enjoyment.
4. I must not treat persons as objects, even in the mind, lest I become a user of persons in practice.
5. Unchaste activity destroys my most precious friendship, that with God, the source of all happiness.
6. Unchaste activity brings pleasure but not happiness.

While some see sex as using someone, a Christian sees sex as a God-given gift in which one gives himself or herself to another in a legitimate marriage, that is, in a covenant of life and love.

Finally, pornography and senseless violence invariably convey a message of disdain for others who are viewed as objects rather than persons. They take a human being as a mere consumer item, as something to enjoy and to play with or to punch. That is, as if she or he was just a bar of chocolate, a toy, or a punching bag. Thus, they take away tenderness and compassion and can foster insensitivity and even brutality. It is also, therefore, important to carefully **monitor the exposure of children to video games,** as some of them contain harmful sexual and violent content. Children should be made to understand that the repeated presentation of violent aggression toward human beings, even when they are presented as criminals, leads to a loss of respect for the dignity of the human person that has been created by God as wearing His image and likeness.

To those who struggle with pornography, we should say: Do not give up! Yes, do not be weary of using or even "diving" to reach for the remote control to change the TV channel, or convey displeasure with a joke, when needed. It is a very formative gesture which is worth a thousand words. It tells everyone that you do not compromise with evil.

While it is true that the young and immature are especially vulnerable and most likely to be victimized by pornography and violence, **no one can consider himself or herself immune to their corrupting effects.** Many of the shows labelled "for adults" are, in fact, immoral, obscene, and degrading. They should not be viewed by anyone, for they are trash! The implication that adults may watch them without any danger of being harmed has been proven false. They, too, are adversely affected, and they, too, offend God, and that is what matters most! What is harmful to the soul of a child is harmful to the soul of an adult.

The testimony of Dr. Judith Reisman, a consultant to the U.S. Department of Justice during three different presidential administrations, who, besides, is the president of the Institute for Media Education in the USA, is very telling in this regard. She said, as reported in *Catholic World Report* (November 2002, p. 40), "*When we have sexually explicit pornography materials in any environment, you get people sexually excited. That's what it is supposed to do, and it does it very well. And when people are sexually excited, they will usually act sexually if they can (...) Sex is not something that is to be distributed like candy. It causes great harm when people are not having their sexual activity in the stricture of a marital relationship. We find people raping people. We find people getting AIDS and dying of venereal diseases (...) Pornography, this massive multi-billion dollar industry, has only one thing at the end of it, and that is destruction and harm.*" And she concludes, saying, "*The big problem here is that we have lost sensibility to sexual offenses.*"

In order to fight pornography, it is important to take into account 1) the **sacredness of human life,** which has an **eternal destiny**; 2) the consequent sacredness of the channels of human life, namely, the sexual powers and organs; 3) and the **immense dignity of the human person,** who, in addition to his great intrinsic worth, has been enabled by Christ to become **a son of God** and **a shrine of the Blessed Trinity.**

a few parting words

I must admit that going through this booklet does not guarantee a chaste life for anyone. Things are not that simple. Our Lord Himself has told us, "*The spirit is willing, but the flesh is weak.*"

And yet, there is a way not to stumble again: To really fall in Love with Jesus Christ. By this I mean, to truly believe, hope, and love Him. St. Josemaría Escrivá says exactly this at the very end of his best seller, *The Way*: "And what is the secret of perseverance? Fall in Love, and you will not leave Him."

Basically, it is a matter of faith. There are some people who question religious doctrine and entertain doubts of faith, not because they find Catholic doctrine intellectually wanting, but because it conflicts with their desires.

If we would *see* Our Lord with our eyes of faith, as a Father attentively looking at us, if we would have presence of God, we would not dare to do anything that offends Him, and we would not want.

Here, the danger lies in thinking that it is enough to love Our Lord a little, holding back a bit, lest taking

Him with excessive seriousness might complicate our lives.

But Jesus is waiting for our **total** commitment. Then, He will give us all the help, all the grace, that we need to be faithful. That is, to be a contemplative, in the midst of the world, who bears in mind that:

"*What is needed for happiness is not a comfortable life, but a heart in love*" (St. Josemaría Escrivá).

About Leonine Publishers

Leonine Publishers LLC makes fine Catholic literature available to Catholics throughout the English-speaking world. Leonine Publishers offers an innovative "hybrid" approach to book publication that helps authors as well as readers. Please visit our web site at www.leoninepublishers.com to learn more about us. Browse our online bookstore to find more solid Catholic titles to uplift, challenge, and inspire.

Our patron and namesake is Pope Leo XIII, a prudent, yet uncompromising pope during the stormy years at the close of the 19th century. Please join us as we ask his intercession for our family of readers and authors.

Do you have a book inside you? Visit our web site today. Leonine Publishers accepts manuscripts from Catholic authors like you. If your book is selected for publication, you will have an active part in the production process. This book is an example of our growing selection of literature for the busy Catholic reader of the 21st century.

www.leoninepublishers.com

www.ingramcontent.com/pod-product-compliance
Lightning Source LLC
La Vergne TN
LVHW050943080826
845145LV00004B/1396

* 9 7 8 1 9 4 2 1 9 0 4 3 1 *